1,000

facts about

WILD
ANIMALS

MOIRA BUTTERFIELD

Kingfisher Books

NEW YORK

Contents

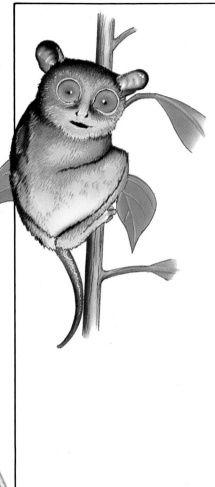

KINGFISHER BOOKS
Grisewood & Dempsey Inc.
95 Madison Avenue
New York, New York 10016

First American edition 1992
10 9 8 7 6 5 4 3
Copyright © Times Four Publishing Ltd. 1992
All rights reserved under International
and Pan-American Copyright Conventions
Produced by Times Four Publishing Ltd.
Designed by Margaret Howdle, Chris Leishman, Brian Robertson
Cover design by Terry Woodley
Additional text contributions by Catriona MacGregor
Illustrated by Michael Steward, Sandra Hill, Ruth Lindsay,
Shelagh McNicholas
Printed in Spain

Library of Congress Cataloging-in-Publication Data
Butterfield, Moira,
Wild animals/Moira Butterfield; [illustrated by Michael Steward
. . . et al.]. – 1st American ed.
p. cm. – (1000 facts about)
Includes index.
Summary: Presents facts about mammals, insects, fish, reptiles,
birds, amphibians, endangered species, and wildlife in the home.
1. Animals–Miscellanea–Juvenile literature. [1. Animals–
Miscellanea.] I. Steward, Michael, ill. II. Title. III. Series.
QL49.B798   1992
591–dc20   92-53114   CIP   AC

ISBN 1–85697–809–5

Introduction

This book is full of interesting facts about the animal kingdom. You can find out what the main animal groups are called and how they are different from each other. Or you can read about animals' homes and habitats, such as deserts, rain forests, and oceans.

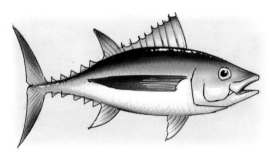

A special section will tell you about the world's endangered animals and the work that is being done to protect them. Find out, too, about some of the unusual and surprising ways that animals behave. There is even a section on some of the wild creatures that may be sharing your own home!

To help you pick out the things you want to read about, some key words are in bold type like this: **reptiles**.

Also, there are lots of easy-to-find facts beginning with a spot, like this:

● Snakes never close their eyes

Across the top of each page there is a list of useful mini-facts — for example, the world's rarest animals, or the most dangerous sea creatures.

On each double page there is a Strange but True section containing especially unusual or startling facts.

On pages 42–45 you will find charts and lists of animals records and facts for you to refer to.

If you are not sure where to find facts about a particular topic, look in the Index on pages 46–48.

The Animal Kingdom

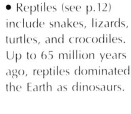

Coelenterates — jellyfish, corals, sea anemones

Animals are creatures that breathe in **oxygen**. They have to **eat** plants or other animals in order to survive.

Animals have been on the Earth in one form or another for about 700 million years. The first animals were tiny single-celled creatures.

Single-celled creatures

Today, several million different kinds of animals live on Earth. Scientists divide them into **related groups**.

Animal groups

Here are the main **animal groups**:

● Mammals (see p.6) include such different examples as bats, whales, cats, kangaroos, and humans. Many large creatures belong to this group.

● Reptiles (see p.12) include snakes, lizards, turtles, and crocodiles. Up to 65 million years ago, reptiles dominated the Earth as dinosaurs.

● Amphibians (see p.12) have bodies that are adapted to live on land or in water. This group includes frogs, toads, newts, and salamanders.

Strange but true

● The present day is sometimes called the "Age of the Insects." Insects vastly outnumber all the other animal groups.

● Because grass give so little nourishment, cows must graze all day to get enough for their needs.

● Some scientists think that apes and humans are descended from a type of rodent, rather like a rat.

Animal food

Animals eat different kinds of **food**, depending on their size, the type of stomach they have, and the food available.

● Animals that eat only plants are called herbivores.

Herbivorous zebra

● Animals that eat both meat and plants are called omnivores.

● Animals that eat only meat are called carnivores.

Carnivorous lion

● Predators help to strengthen the animal population. They tend to catch and kill the weakest members of an animal group. The strongest ones are left alive. These are more likely to breed healthy offspring.

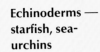
● Fish (see p.10) are a large group of underwater creatures. This group includes such varied examples as sharks, seahorses, and eels.

● The bird group (see p.14) includes many different flying birds and some non-flying kinds. Examples of this group are found all over the world.

● Insects (see p.8) are by far the largest group of animals in the world today. They include ants, beetles, bees, butterflies, lice, and flies.

● Arachnids have eight legs, in contrast to the six-legged insects. The arachnid group includes scorpions, harvestmen, mites, and spiders.

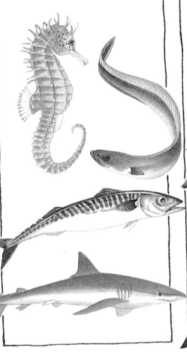

The food chain

Animals are linked together by what they eat, forming a **food chain**. The smallest animals eat plants. They are in turn eaten by larger animals, and so on. Here is a typical food chain:

Bird of prey (the end of this chain)

Plant (eaten by aphid)

Spider (eaten by small bird)

Small bird (eaten by bird of prey)

Aphid (eaten by spider)

Mouse (eaten by bird of prey)

Mammals

Mammals are a very successful group of animals found all over the world. There are about **4,050 species** in all.

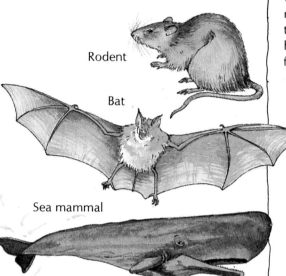

Rodent

Bat

Sea mammal

The mammal family includes **bats**, **rodents** (small gnawing creatures such as rats and mice), and some sea animals such as **whales** and **dolphins**. It also includes **primates**. Human beings are part of the primate group, along with lemurs, monkeys, and apes.

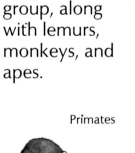

Primates

Mammal facts

Mammals have:

● Hairy bodies, to help them keep warm. Some mammals have thick fur; some only have a fine fur.

● Skulls and backbones. Animals with backbones are called vertebrates.

● Warm blood, which means that they can keep their own body temperature at a comfortable level.

● The ability to suckle their young, which means that they can feed babies with milk from their body.

Different kinds of mammal

Zoologists split mammals into three **scientific groups**. Each group gives birth to babies in a different way.

● Monotremes lay eggs and hatch their young. There are only two types of monotremes: the duck-billed platypus from Australia and the spiny anteaters or echidnas from Australia and New Guinea.

Duck-billed platypus

● Marsupial mammal babies are born very tiny and undeveloped. Most marsupial babies finish growing inside pouches on their mother's body. Kangaroos are marsupials.

● Placental mammal babies are born alive and well-developed. When a placental baby is growing inside its mother it lives inside a kind of protective sac. Its blood supply is linked to its mother s.

A human embryo

Baby in pouch

Amazing mammals

Mammals are lots of different shapes and sizes. That is partly because they have developed to survive in many different kinds of places. Here are some **mammal record-breakers**:

• The world's noisiest land animals are South American howler monkeys. When the male monkeys call, their screams can be heard from 10 miles (16 km) away.

• The world's largest land mammal is the African elephant. Adult bull elephants grow over 10 feet (3 m) tall and weigh about 6 tons.

• Cheetahs are the world's fastest animals on land. They can run up to 60 mph (100 km/h) over short distances.

• The giraffe is the tallest mammal in the world. It can grow over 16 feet (5 m). It has a long neck so that it can reach leaves high up in the trees.

Primates

Primates are the most well-developed mammals. They have:

• Complex brains, which means that they are able to think better than most other creatures in the animal kingdom.

• The ability to stand upright for long periods.

• More highly-developed hands than any other animal group. They can use their hands for all kinds of complicated skills.

• Eyes set side by side in the front of the head, which means that they can see more clearly than most other creatures.

Strange but true

• Many mammals sleep for long periods. Lions sleep up to 20 hours a day.

• Gorillas sleep in nests which they build in low branches of trees.

• Lions and tigers have been successfully crossed to make a new animal — the "tigon."

• Blue whale babies weigh up to 7 tons (7,000 kg) at birth.

7

Insects

These insects are dangerous to crops or humans:

Tsetse fly (hot climates) — spreads sleeping sickness

Insects are the biggest animal group. There are vast numbers of them, and there are probably many unknown types of insect still to be discovered.

Insects are found all over the world, even in frozen lands and in scorching deserts where other animals find it hard to survive.

Most insects live on their own for most of their lives, but some insects, such as bees, live in **organized communities** with many companions of the same type.

Insect parts

Insects do not all look the same, but they all have some characteristics in common. **All insects** have:

- A protective outer covering called an "exoskeleton." Insects are "invertebrates," which means that they do not have backbones. They do have internal skeletons.

- A head which carries the eyes, antennae, and feeding parts.

- An abdomen, made up of a series of segments. Vital organs such as the heart are inside.

- A thorax, which carries legs and sometimes wings.

- Three pairs of jointed legs.

- Cold blood, which means that they cannot control their own body temperature. They rely on the temperature of their surroundings to keep them alive.

- Many insects have compound eyes, made of hundreds of tiny lenses.

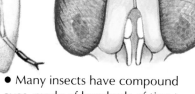

Head
Thorax
Eye
Abdomen

Strange but true

- Some butterflies have scented wings, to attract a mate.

- Some insects produce tiny lights on their bodies to attract mates.

- Crickets have ears positioned on their knees.

- Prehistoric dragonflies had wingspans up to 30 inches (76 cm) across, wider than many modern birds.

Growing up

Some insects go through a complete change of body and appearance called **metamorphosis**. There are four stages:

1. The female insect lays lots of tiny eggs, sometimes on the underside of a leaf.

2. The eggs hatch into larvae. Caterpillars, grubs, and maggots are all forms of insect larvae.

3. When the larva has grown enough it changes into a pupa (or chrysalis), inside a hard case called a cocoon, the insect's body dissolves and reforms into a new shape.

4. Once the change has occurred, the cocoon splits open and the adult insect comes out. Butterflies, moths, beetles, flies, ants, and bees all go through metamorphosis.

Types of insect

The **insect world** is divided into groups. Here are some of them:

Cricket

● Crickets and grasshoppers have strong hind legs for jumping. They can rub parts of the body together to make a "singing" sound that attracts a mate.

Honey bees

● Wasps and bees live in well-organized communities, where each insect has a particular job to do.

Dragonfly

● Dragonflies and damselflies have fierce jaws which they use to catch other flying insects such as flies.

● Bugs are insects with mouthparts made for sucking. Some bugs feed on plant juices; some feed on blood.

● Flies have only one pair of wings, but they also have tiny balancing organs at the back of their bodies. These help them to land upside down.

Blackfly bug

● Some bugs live in or on water. You can often see them walking over the surfaces of ponds.

● Beetles are the biggest insect group. Their front wings are hard outer coverings for their back wings.

Stag beetle

Water strider

● Butterflies and moths have tiny scales that cover their bodies. The scales are made up of thousands of tiny hairs.

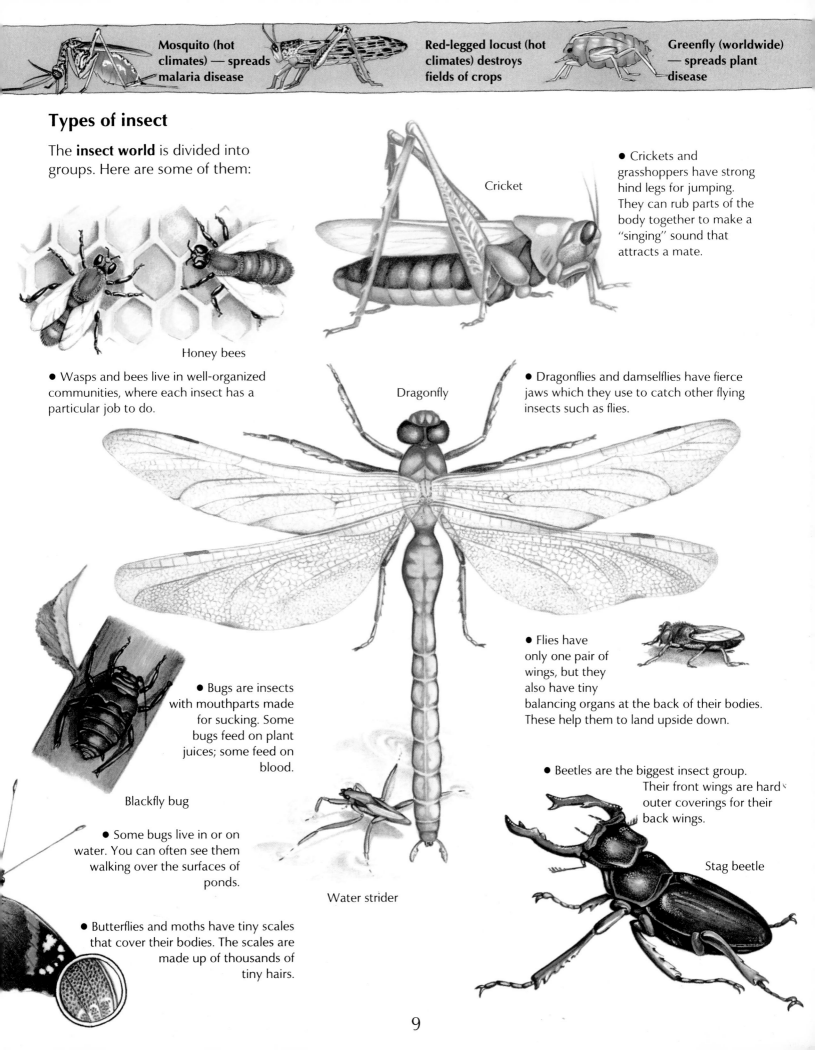

9

Fish

Fish are used to make these products:

Glue (contains boiled-down fish bones)

Fish live in oceans, rivers, lakes, and ponds. They are **cold-blooded**, which means that they cannot change their own body temperature.

There are about 20,000 different **species**, ranging from giant whale sharks about 40 feet (12 m) long to dwarf gobies no bigger than a thumbnail.

Bony fish

Most fish belong to the **bony fish** group, which means that they have **bone skeletons** inside their bodies. Many of the fish we eat are of this kind.

• Bony fish have a gill slit on either side of the body. The slits are covered over with flaps of skin.

• Flat fish, such as flounders, are bony. They lie on one side of their bodies.

Jawless fish

Lampreys and hagfish belong to the **jawless** fish group.

• Jawless fish have round sucking funnels for mouths. They have sharp teeth to hook onto their prey.

• Lampreys suck the blood of prey. Hagfish eat the flesh of their victims.

• Most bony fish have a little air-filled sac called a swim bladder inside their bodies. This bladder acts rather like water wings; it keeps the fish floating in the water.

Fish facts

Most fish have:

• Backbones. All fish are vertebrates.

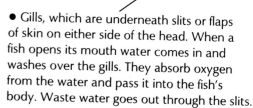

• A scaly skin, which stays moist and waterproof. Eels and lampreys are the only fish to have smooth skins.

• Gills, which are underneath slits or flaps of skin on either side of the head. When a fish opens its mouth water comes in and washes over the gills. They absorb oxygen from the water and pass it into the fish's body. Waste water goes out through the slits.

Strange but true

• Pufferfish can puff their bodies up to scare away enemies.

• Salmon live in the sea, but they return to breed in the river where they were born.

• There are probably about a quintillion herring in the Atlantic Ocean (a million million million).

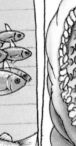

• A female cod can lay up to 9 million eggs.

Jawless fish mouth

Lamprey

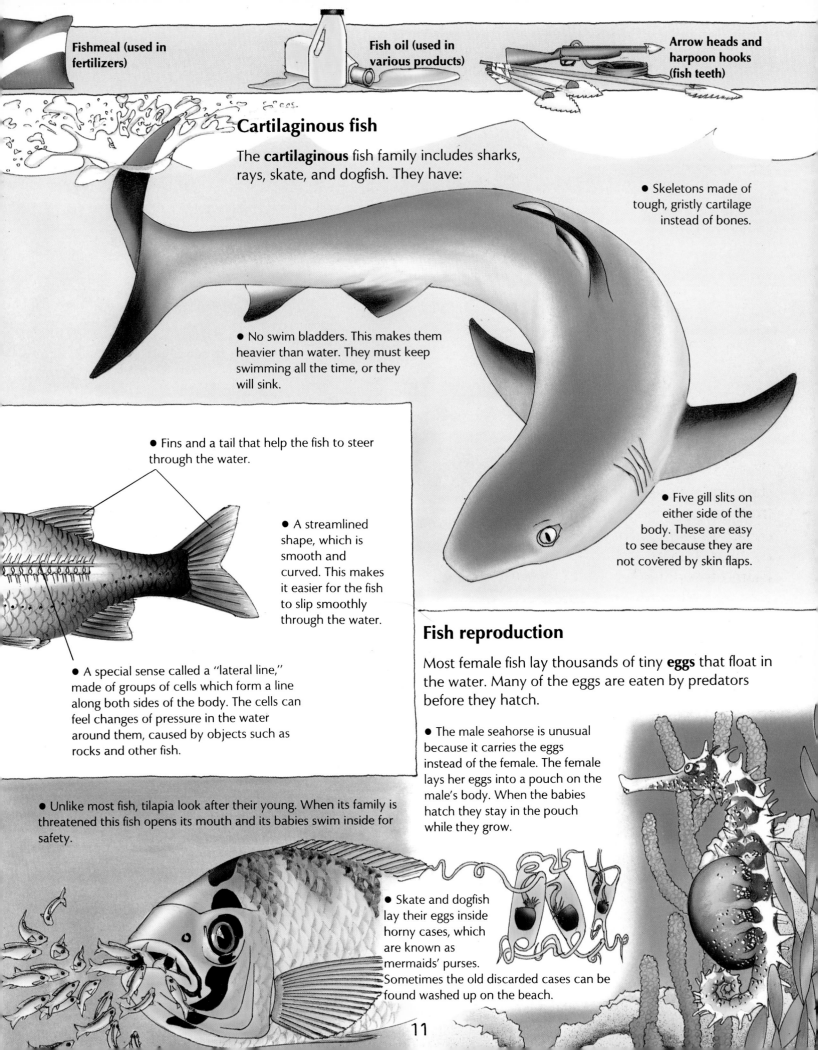

Fishmeal (used in fertilizers)

Fish oil (used in various products)

Arrow heads and harpoon hooks (fish teeth)

Cartilaginous fish

The **cartilaginous** fish family includes sharks, rays, skate, and dogfish. They have:

● Skeletons made of tough, gristly cartilage instead of bones.

● No swim bladders. This makes them heavier than water. They must keep swimming all the time, or they will sink.

● Fins and a tail that help the fish to steer through the water.

● A streamlined shape, which is smooth and curved. This makes it easier for the fish to slip smoothly through the water.

● Five gill slits on either side of the body. These are easy to see because they are not covered by skin flaps.

● A special sense called a "lateral line," made of groups of cells which form a line along both sides of the body. The cells can feel changes of pressure in the water around them, caused by objects such as rocks and other fish.

Fish reproduction

Most female fish lay thousands of tiny **eggs** that float in the water. Many of the eggs are eaten by predators before they hatch.

● The male seahorse is unusual because it carries the eggs instead of the female. The female lays her eggs into a pouch on the male's body. When the babies hatch they stay in the pouch while they grow.

● Unlike most fish, tilapia look after their young. When its family is threatened this fish opens its mouth and its babies swim inside for safety.

● Skate and dogfish lay their eggs inside horny cases, which are known as mermaids' purses. Sometimes the old discarded cases can be found washed up on the beach.

Reptiles and Amphibians

Amphibians are a group of animals that spend part of their lives in water and part of their lives on land. **Frogs**, **toads**, **newts**, and **salamanders** are all examples.

Amphibians

Amphibians

Amphibians have moist **slimy skin**. They always live near **fresh water** because they must return there in order to breed.

- There are swimming frogs, burrowing frogs, climbing frogs, and even flying frogs that can glide from tree to tree.

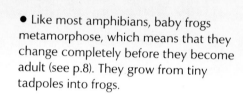

- Like most amphibians, baby frogs metamorphose, which means that they change completely before they become adult (see p.8). They grow from tiny tadpoles into frogs.

Spawn   Tadpole   Legs form   Frog

Reptiles live and breed mostly on land, although a few live in water. **Snakes**, **lizards**, **crocodiles**, and **turtles** are all reptiles.

Reptiles

Reptiles

Reptiles are **cold-blooded**, which is why they need to live in warm climates. They have scaly, **waterproof skin** and most of them lay **eggs** with tough protective shells.

Lizards are reptiles with scaly bodies and four limbs:

- Some lizards have collars of skin which they puff out to make themselves look bigger when they are excited or scared.

Frilled lizard

Tortoises, **terrapins**, and **turtles** are reptiles with protective shells.

- Turtles live in seawater. They only come ashore to lay their eggs.

- The largest, heaviest lizard is the komodo dragon from Indonesia. It can grow up to 10 feet (3 m) long, and is a fierce hunter.

Komodo dragon

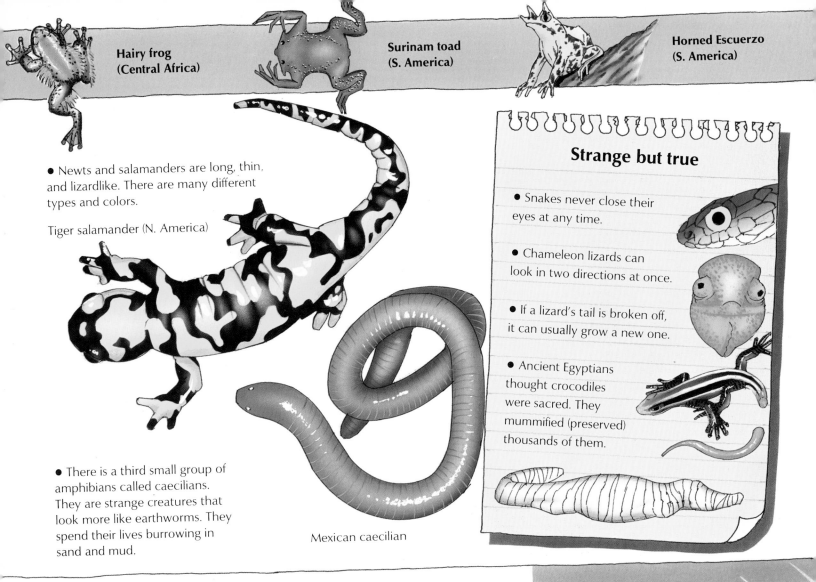

Hairy frog
(Central Africa)

Surinam toad
(S. America)

Horned Escuerzo
(S. America)

• Newts and salamanders are long, thin, and lizardlike. There are many different types and colors.

Tiger salamander (N. America)

• There is a third small group of amphibians called caecilians. They are strange creatures that look more like earthworms. They spend their lives burrowing in sand and mud.

Mexican caecilian

Strange but true

• Snakes never close their eyes at any time.

• Chameleon lizards can look in two directions at once.

• If a lizard's tail is broken off, it can usually grow a new one.

• Ancient Egyptians thought crocodiles were sacred. They mummified (preserved) thousands of them.

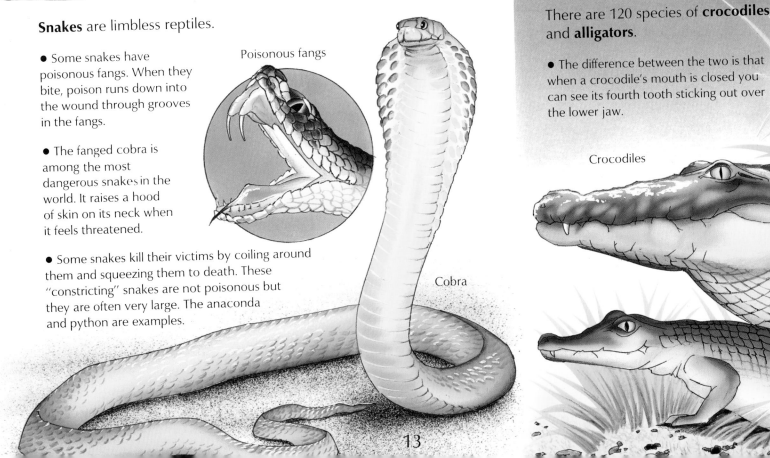

Snakes are limbless reptiles.

• Some snakes have poisonous fangs. When they bite, poison runs down into the wound through grooves in the fangs.

• The fanged cobra is among the most dangerous snakes in the world. It raises a hood of skin on its neck when it feels threatened.

• Some snakes kill their victims by coiling around them and squeezing them to death. These "constricting" snakes are not poisonous but they are often very large. The anaconda and python are examples.

Poisonous fangs

Cobra

There are 120 species of **crocodiles** and **alligators**.

• The difference between the two is that when a crocodile's mouth is closed you can see its fourth tooth sticking out over the lower jaw.

Crocodiles

Birds

Birds are **warm-blooded** animals with **internal skeletons**. They all have **wings** and **feathers**, although not all birds can fly. There is a wide variety of birds. They live in many different habitats all over the world, from icy polar lands to hot tropical rain forests. Some birds live alone or in small groups. Others live in **colonies** numbering many thousands.

Bird facts

Most birds have bodies designed for flight. All **flying birds** have these physical features:

● A light, waterproof covering of feathers over most of the body. They help birds to fly and also keep body heat in, so the bird stays warm.

● A streamlined body shape. This helps birds to travel smoothly through the air by cutting down air resistance.

● Two wings covered with extra-strong flight feathers. The wings help to raise the bird into the air and the bird keeps itself aloft by flapping them.

● A horny pointed beak for feeding. Different birds have differently shaped beaks.

● Lightweight, partly hollow internal bones.

● Scaly legs and feet with three or four toes and sharp claws.

Strange but true

● The earliest known bird, called Archaeopteryx, lived 150 million years ago. Unlike modern birds it had teeth.

● Swifts spend almost all their lives in the air. They only land to breed.

● Flamingoes are pink because their bodies take on the pink color of the shrimps they eat.

● The Andean sword-billed hummingbird has a beak longer than its body.

Eggs and nests

Bird species breed at certain times of the year, when the weather is mild and there is a good supply of food.

● Some male birds use complicated dances, special songs, or displays to attract females. For instance, the male peacock shows off its bright tail feathers to interest a mate.

Peacock male

● Eggs vary in color and shape. For instance, some are speckled so that they are difficult to spot when they are lying in a nest.

Types of bird

Here are some different **bird groups**:

Osprey with fish

● Birds of prey (also called raptors) hunt other animals. They have curved talons for grasping prey, hooked beaks for tearing flesh, and good eyesight to help them hunt. Eagles, owls, and hawks are all birds of prey.

African ostrich

● Some bird species have lost the ability to fly. The world's largest bird, the African ostrich, is an example. It is too heavy to take off but it has powerful legs and can run as fast as 40 mph (65 km/h).

Feathers

Bird feathers are made from **keratin**, a substance which is also found in hair and horn.

● Down the middle of a feather there is a stiff horny shaft called a quill.

● The flat part on either side of the quill is called the vane. It is made from tiny fibers called barbs. There are about 600 barbs on either side, each carrying smaller offshoots. All the barbs and offshoots are locked tightly together by hooks to make a smooth surface.

Quill

Vane

Barbs

● Water birds have long legs for wading. They often have webbed feet to help them paddle, and long bills or beaks for finding food in the water. Cormorants, ducks, and flamingos are examples of waterbirds.

Weaver bird's nest

● Most birds build nests where they lay eggs and hatch young. One of the most complicated examples is the carefully woven bell-shaped nest of the weaver bird, found in Africa and Australia.

A colony of flamingos

Grassland Animals

Grasslands are wide, open areas where grasses and shrubs grow.

Temperate grasslands are found in cool parts of the world in the middle of large land masses, where rainfall is low. These areas are often used for cattle.

Tropical grassland is found mainly in Africa and South America. In Africa it is called **savanna**, and in South America it is called **pampas**. Here rain falls only in summer.

Tropical grassland provides a home for many wild animals.

Plant-eating animals

Most grassland animals are **grazers**, eating grass and other plants. Grazers live together in **herds**, for safety. They move about looking for fresh pastures and water pools. Here are some examples of plant-eaters on the **African savanna**:

● Antelope live in most tropical grassland areas. Species include orynx, eland, and gazelles. Although they are only 2 feet (60 cm) tall, gazelles can run at 55 mph (90 km/h) to escape danger.

● The African savanna has shrubs and trees as well as grass. These provide food for giraffes, elephants, and rhino.

● Zebras move in large herds, often accompanied by wildebeest. While some zebras graze, others stay on the lookout for lions, their main enemy. Zebras can hear and smell better than most other grazing creatures.

Strange but true

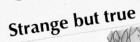

● Elephants spend 23 hours a day eating.

● Some antelope can leap 10 feet (3 m) in the air from a standing start.

● Vultures sometimes eat so much they can't take off again.

● No two zebras have exactly the same pattern of stripes. Like human fingerprints, each zebra pattern is unique.

Zebras prefer taller grasses

Some antelope stand on their hind legs to reach low tree branches

Giraffes and elephants eat the tops of trees

Meat-eaters

The main threat to the grassland plant-eaters are **meat-eaters** such as lions, leopards, and hunting dogs.

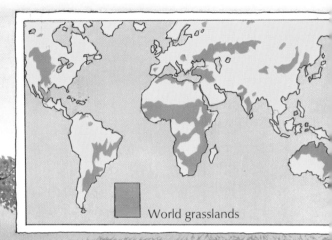

World grasslands

- Lions live in groups called prides. They hunt and kill only when they are hungry. Antelope and zebras are their favorite food.

- African hunting dogs live in large, well-organized packs. They hunt together, separating weak or young animals from herds.

Scavengers

Scavengers are creatures who eat the leftovers from dead animal carcasses. When the grassland hunters have finished with their prey, the scavengers move in to pick the bones clean.

- Vultures are large birds found in many grassland areas of the world. They use their keen eyesight to spot dead animals far below them.

- Hyenas usually eat the remains of another animal's kill, but they will hunt if food is scarce. Their "chuckling" hunting cry sounds rather like a human laugh.

- Although vultures and hyenas have a bad reputation, they provide a useful "garbage disposal" service, because if carcasses are left to rot they attract flies and disease.

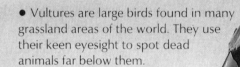

Rain forests are hot, steamy jungles that grow in areas on either side of the equator — an imaginary line that circles the middle of the Earth. Rain forest areas have **high temperatures** and **heavy rainfall** all the year round. They are the richest animal and plant habitats in the world.

Equator

Rain forest area

Strange but true

- The African jungle okapi's tongue is so long, it can be used to lick the creature's eyes.

- The African giant snail grows up to 15 inches (39 cm) long.

- The strongest-known animal poison comes from the arrow-poison frog.

- The Amazon "Jesus Christ lizard" can run across water.

Rain forest birds

Many **birds** make their home in the rain forest trees.

Hornbill

- Each forest region has its own giant eagle species. These birds build huge twig platforms on top of the highest trees.

Toucan

- Brightly-colored macaws, hornbills, and toucans make their nests in holes in tree trunks.

Macaw

- There are lots of different hummingbird species in the Amazon region. They hover by flowers, drinking the sweet nectar with their long beaks.

Hummingbird

Rain forest insects

There are many, many thousands of different insect species in the rain forests.

- Ants can be found everywhere in the rain forests. Huge columns of fierce army ants travel through the forest areas of Central America, destroying everything in their path.

- Giant butterflies flit among the trees. Many of them are brightly-colored. This is a signal that they taste horrible.

18

Monkey-eating eagle —
Philippines

Golden lion marmoset —
South America

Orangutan —
Sumatra

Animals in the trees

Most rain forest **mammals** live up in the tree branches.

● The Amazon sloth hangs motionless and upside down for days on end. It has a shaggy coat and long claws for gripping branches.

Sloth

Gliders

● The Asian flying squirrel glides from tree to tree using the skin stretched between its legs like a parachute.

Flying squirrel

Flying snake

● When the flying snake launches itself, it flattens its body into a broad ribbon shape so that it can glide through the air.

Margay

● There are lots of different jungle monkeys. Some of them have prehensile tails, which can be used like a hand to grip onto things.

● The Amazon margay and the ocelot are types of rain forest cat. Both are expert tree climbers.

Ocelot

Reptiles

Rain forests make ideal homes for warmth-loving **reptiles**.

● The world's biggest insect, the Goliath beetle, lives in African rain forests.

● The bushmaster snake lives among tree branches. It has heat-sensitive patches on its head, so it can find possible victims by sensing their body heat. Its bite can kill humans.

● The world's heaviest snake is the anaconda, found in South America and Trinidad. It can weigh up to 330 pounds (150 kg), and strangles its prey by coiling around it. It feeds mainly on birds, deer, and rodents.

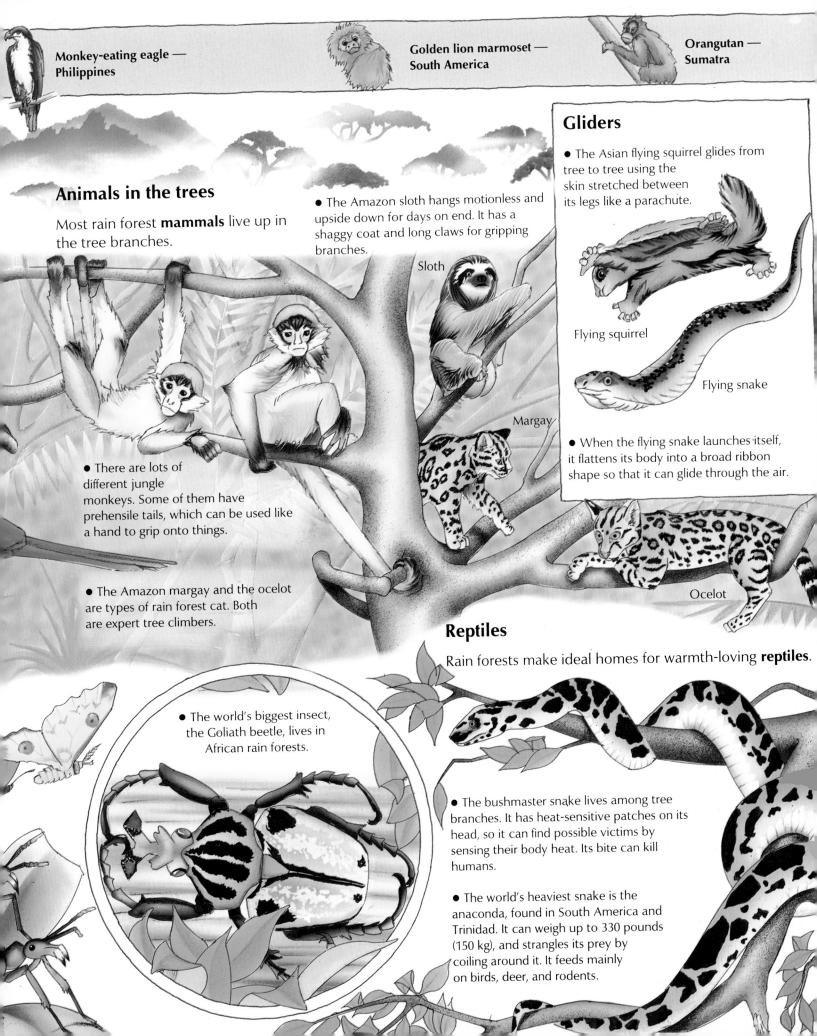

Desert Animals

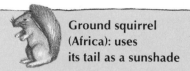
About one eighth of the Earth's surface is **desert**. A desert is an area where less than 10 inches (25 cm) of rain falls on average each year.

Some deserts are very cold in winter. Others are hot all the year round, with high temperatures during the day and cooler temperatures at night.

Most desert animals tend to come out at night, staying out of the daytime heat by sheltering under rocks or in their underground burrows.

The major problem of desert survival is **lack of water**. Many animals are cleverly adapted to cope with the drought.

Strange but true

- Crocodile tracks have been found in the middle of the Sahara Desert.

- Prehistoric rock paintings in the Sahara show giraffes, antelope, and elephants. None of these animals live in the region today.

- Australian farmers once called in the army to wage an "emu war" on Outback desert emus who came on to farms and destroyed crops.

Snakes and lizards

Snakes and **lizards** are cold-blooded (see p.12) and need the Sun's heat in order to survive. Deserts are ideal homes for them.

Rattlesnake

- There are many different kinds of American rattlesnake, most of them highly poisonous. When a rattlesnake is angry, it makes a warning rattle by shaking scales positioned on the end of its tail.

- Sidewinder snakes have developed an efficient way of traveling over soft sand. They use their bodies to lever themselves along, leaving trails of wavy lines behind them on the sand.

Sidewinder snake

Amphibians

- The American spadefoot toad burrows underground during hot weather. It can stay buried for up to 11 months because its waterproof coat keeps moisture in its body. When rain arrives, the toads come out to breed.

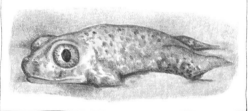

Insects and spiders

There are many different **desert insects** and **spiders**.

- When it rains, the eggs of bugs, beetles, and butterflies hatch, after lying dormant for many months.

- Most desert spiders are hunters. They do not use webs to trap prey. Instead they search for creatures to attack.

- A Namib Desert darkling beetle collects water from sea fog that rolls in from the nearby Atlantic. The fog condenses on the beetle's body and runs into its mouth.

Darkling beetle

Red-kneed tarantula (Mexico)

Desert mammals

Desert mammals usually stay out of the daytime heat, in order to conserve water. Many of the smaller mammals never drink, getting all the moisture they need from seeds, shoots, or other creatures.

● The Saharan fennec fox has especially big ears that help to keep it cool. Blood vessels run near the skin surface of the ears, giving off heat as air blows across them.

Saharan fennec fox

Kangaroo rat

● The most common desert mammals are rodents. The kangaroo rat is an example. It stores plant seeds deep in its burrow, leaving them to collect moisture from the soil. This way, the rat gets a ready supply of water.

● Camels can survive for many days without regular water or food. They have wide, hairy feet to stop them sinking in the sand, and their nostrils can close up to keep out dust.

One-humped dromedary

Desert birds

Most **desert birds** shelter from the daytime heat beneath rocks or plants.

● The saguaro cactus is found in the Sonoran desert in southwest U.S.A. It can grow up to 50 feet (15 m) high, and provides a home for several desert birds. Gila woodpeckers peck out nest holes in the rubbery cactus flesh. Tiny elf owls nest in vacant holes and cactus wrens nest in forks.

● The emu is found in Australian desert regions. It is the world's second largest bird (after the ostrich). It grows up to 5½ feet (1.7 m) high, and although it cannot fly it can run up to 40 mph (64 km/h) over short distances.

● Roadrunners are found in Mexico and Arizona. They are famous for their speed. They can run up to 23 mph (37 km/h) to catch snakes and lizards.

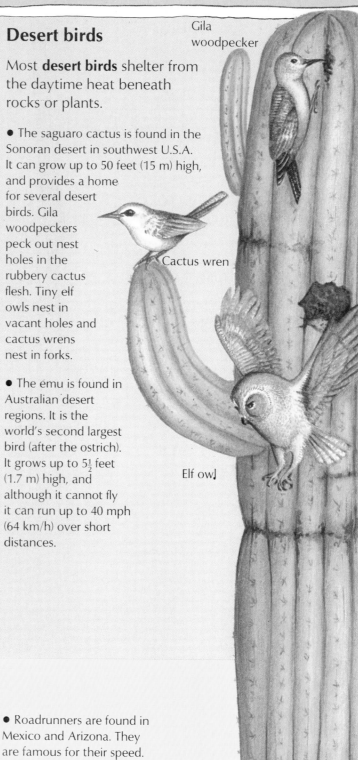
Gila woodpecker

Cactus wren

Elf owl

Roadrunner

Northern Forest Animals

In northern parts of the world there are areas of cool forest which provide a home for all sorts of different creatures.

There are two types of cool forest. In warmer areas the trees are mainly deciduous, which means they shed their leaves in winter. In cold areas the trees are mainly coniferous, which means they have long-lasting needles instead of leaves.

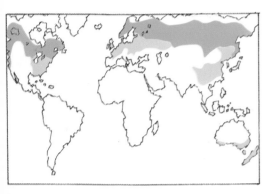

Coniferous forest

Deciduous forest

Many forest creatures are very shy and will hide if they hear strange noises. A good time to spot forest wildlife is at dusk or very early in the morning, when the animals tend to feed.

Deciduous woods

Deciduous trees have widely-spread branches. The gaps between their leaves allow plenty of sunlight through to the forest floor, where lots of plants grow and provide food for animals.

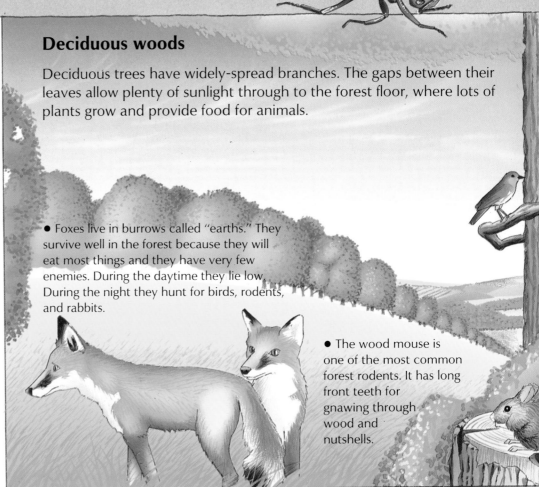

● Foxes live in burrows called "earths." They survive well in the forest because they will eat most things and they have very few enemies. During the daytime they lie low. During the night they hunt for birds, rodents, and rabbits.

● The wood mouse is one of the most common forest rodents. It has long front teeth for gnawing through wood and nutshells.

Coniferous forests

Tree in coniferous forests are densely packed together. Very little light penetrates to the poor soil beneath, so there are few small plants. There is less animal life than in deciduous forests because there is less to eat.

● Martens have long bodies and short legs. There are several different species, including the pine marten.

Pine marten

● Red deer are common in northern forests. Male deer (stags) have long antlers covered in soft velvet. Each year the antlers drop off and a new pair grows.

Woodlouse

Centipede

Pill millipede

Snail

Bark beetle

- Lots of different insect-eating birds find food amongst the trees.

- Badgers are timid night time creatures. They can see well in the dark and have a strong sense of smell, so it is difficult to watch them without disturbing them.

- Caterpillars and insects feed off the tree leaves, while bark beetles bore into the trucks.

- Wild rabbits live in large groups in complicated tunnel networks called "warrens."

- Woodpeckers have strong beaks for drilling nest holes in tree trunks. They can sometimes be heard hammering on wood.

- A squirrel can leap 13 to 16 feet (4 to 5 m) from branch to branch quite effortlessly, using its powerful hind legs to launch itself into the air. It uses its outstretched tail like a rudder, to steer its flight.

Strange but true

- The woodpecker has an extra-strong shock-resistant skull.

- Wood ants squirt powerful formic acid at their enemies.

- Male stags must not be approached when they call during the mating season, as they are liable to attack anyone nearby, mistaking them for a rival.

- Squirrels sometimes wrap their bushy tails around themselves to keep warm.

23

Mountain Animals

Chinchilla
(S. America)

Some animals are adapted to survive the harsh weather conditions often found in **mountains**.

The higher you go, the colder and wetter the climate becomes. Mountain animals tend to have **thick furry coats** or **extra layers of fat** to keep them warm.

Rocky Mountain goat

Mountain animals

• Yaks have long, thick coats to keep them warm in the Himalayan Mountains in Tibet. Sometimes they graze at heights above 15,000 feet (4,500 m), making them the highest-living land animals.

Yak

• Llamas and vicuna belong to the camel family. They are farmed for wool and meat by the Quechua Indians high up in the Andean mountains of South America.

Llama

• The spectacled bear lives in the Andes Mountains. It gets its name from round facial markings.

Spectacled bear

• The Apollo butterfly lives high up in mountainous regions across the world. Spiders are found high up, too. However, it is usually too cold for reptiles and amphibians to survive.

Apollo butterfly

• Cougars (also called pumas or panthers) live in the mountain forests of America. They are very strong, powerful animals and can travel hundreds of miles a week in search of food.

Cougar

• Rocky Mountain goats are experts at climbing steep rocks. They have hoof pads which give them extra grip and allow them to climb up almost vertical surfaces. Their toes are shaped like pincers to help them get a firm footing.

• The chamois goat can climb very quickly. It has been known to climb over 3,200 feet (1,000 m) in 15 minutes.

Chamois

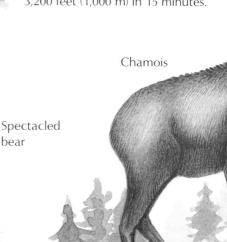

Strange but true

• The cougar can jump as high as 16 feet (5 m) from a standing position.

• High in the mountains the level of oxygen in the air gets less, so some animals have larger hearts and lungs than normal, to compensate.

• A griffon vulture once crashed into an aircraft at the amazing height of 35,400 feet (10,800 m) above ground level.

24

Red panda
(Himalayas)

Snow leopard
(Asia)

Marmot
(N. America,
Eurasia)

• The bobcat hunts
small animals in
the mountainous
regions of North
America and
Mexico. During the
breeding season it
makes eerie
screaming sounds.

Bobcat

High flyers

Many mountain birds are **raptors**, or birds
of prey (see p.15).

• The Andean condor is the world's
largest bird of prey, weighing as much as
26 pounds (12 kg). It has a wingspan
of about 10 feet (3 m). Like its
relatives the vultures, it is
a scavenger, which means
it feeds on animal
carcasses (see p.17).

Andean condor

Golden eagle

Coping in the cold

In the winter months, when the
weather is at its fiercest and food
is hard to find, some mountain
animals **hibernate**, which means
that they sleep deeply for a long
time. During hibernation:

• Body temperature drops.

Hibernating
mountain
hare

• The animal's heartbeat slows down,
so that it uses up less energy.

• The body's fat reserves are gradually
used up for nutrition.

• Eagles can fly very high. They glide on
warm air currents called thermals to help
lift them higher. Remains of Steppe eagles
have been found on Mount Everest at heights
of 25,000 feet (7,500 m). It is thought that
some eagles even fly right over Mount Everest.

Polar Animals

At the far south of the Earth there is a large area of land called **Antarctica**. It is always frozen over with ice.

Most Antarctic animals are **seabirds** and **ocean creatures** such as seals and fish.

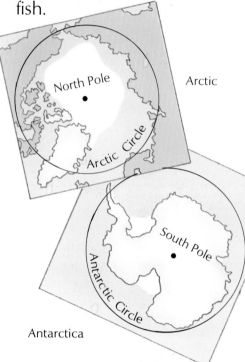

North Pole

Arctic

Arctic Circle

Antarctica

South Pole

Antarctic Circle

The **Arctic** is the area at the far north of the Earth. The Arctic Ocean is in the middle, covered by a huge floating sheet of ice.

Within the Arctic Circle there is barren land called **tundra**, where most of the Arctic animals live.

Arctic tundra animals

Most animals only come to the Arctic tundra during the short **summer months** and **migrate south** when winter comes. A few species brave the winter blizzards. Some of them burrow underground to wait for warmer temperatures in spring.

● Musk oxen are gentle creatures with warm, shaggy coats. They live in family groups which wander the tundra grazing on grasses. They stay on the tundra in winter.

● In summer, big herds of caribou (also called reindeer) travel up to the tundra from North America and Scandinavia.

Caribou

Musk oxen

● Lemmings are the commonest small tundra animals. They are part of the rodent family. They live in underground burrows during winter and come up to the surface to feed in summer.

Lemming

● Polar bears are the fiercest Arctic animals. They stay all year round, hunting for seals. They can swim and dive well and they can sniff the scent of prey from several miles away. Male polar bears spend most of the time on their own. Female bears look after their cubs for a year or so.

Polar bears

Arctic whales

● Bowheads are baleen whales. Instead of teeth they have curtains of bony strips. As a whale swims along, the strips sieve the water, collecting tiny shrimplike krill to eat.

● The beluga is a toothed whale, so it doesn't rely on krill for its food. It feeds on fish at the floe edge, which is the place where the Arctic pack ice meets the sea.

Narwhal

● Male narwhals grow long spiraling tusks. They are sometimes nicknamed sea unicorns.

Beluga

Bowhead

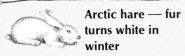
Arctic hare — fur turns white in winter

Seals — lots of fat to keep the cold out

Arctic fox — small body to limit heat loss

Arctic birds

Lots of **seabirds** migrate to the Arctic in summer.

● More than half a million seabird pairs nest in summer on the cliffs of Prince Leopold Island, in the Canadian Arctic.

Seabird

Antarctic animals

Since most of the Antarctic is covered in ice, there are very few land animals. But the oceans are rich in **fish**, **squid**, and **krill**, providing plenty of food for other sea creatures. In the Antarctic Ocean region there are:

● Fish that produce a natural kind of antifreeze to protect themselves from the extremely cold temperatures underwater.

Antarctic fish

● Seven different types of Antarctic seal. They swim under the ice and saw through it with their teeth to make breathing holes that go up to the surface.

Crabeater seal

● Blue whales, the world's biggest and heaviest living creatures. They can grow up to 100 feet (30 m) long. They feed through baleen plates.

● Very few inland animals. The only ones are flies, mites, lice, fleas, and tiny microbes. Mites are the most southerly-living animals on Earth.

Blue whale

Albatross

● Giant albatross seabirds, which come to the Antarctic coast to breed. They can live for up to 70 or 80 years.

● Several different types of penguin. The biggest one is the emperor penguin, which breeds in large colonies.

Strange but true

● The biggest Antarctic inland animal is a wingless fly measuring about $2\frac{1}{2}$ inches (60 mm) long.

● Antarctic squid can grow up to 65 feet (20 m) long. Many of them are cannibals — they attack and eat other squid.

Arctic seals

Seals sit on the Arctic ice floes or swim in the ocean looking for fish to eat.

Ringed seal

Bearded seal

Emperor penguin with chick

Undersea Animals

These fish are poisonous:

Lionfish: poisonous spines

The **oceans** provide one of the largest wildlife habitats in the world. They cover about 70 percent of the Earth's surface, and animals live in almost every part.

Ocean communities vary depending on the temperature and depth of the sea. Animals that live near the water surface are quite different from those that live deeper down.

Coral reefs and seaweed forests provide specialized habitats for particular kinds of creatures.

Ocean food

Ocean creatures have their own **food chain** (see p.5):

- The food chain begins with tiny floating plants called phytoplankton. They float around in the seawater, near the surface. They are eaten by microscopic floating creatures called zooplankton.

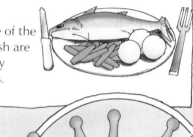

Magnified zooplankton

- The zooplankton are eaten by small fish, which often travel around in groups called shoals.

- Baleen whales bypass part of the food chain and eat zooplankton (see p.26).

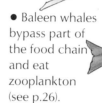

- The small fish are eaten in their turn by larger fish, such as tuna.

- Some of the larger fish are eaten by humans.

Coral reefs

Coral reefs are made up of many thousands of individual animals called **polyps**. There are two kinds of corals: **hard** and **soft**.

A coral polyp

- A coral polyp is a cylinder-shaped animal with a ring of tentacles. It takes calcium carbonate from the water and makes it into limestone.

- Hard corals build up a hard wall of limestone around themselves. As the polyps grow and increase, a reef grows.

- Soft corals have a soft layer of tissue on the outside of a central rod.

Stingray: poisonous
tail spine

Stonefish: poisonous
spines

Blue-ringed octopus:
deadly bite

Unusual fish

Here are some examples of **unusual ocean fish**:

• The sawfish is found in warm oceans.
It has a long flattened snout with
toothed edges. As the fish moves along,
it swings its saw from side to side,
stunning and wounding small fish
which it then eats. It is
harmless to humans.

Sawfish

Bridal burrfish

• The wobbegong is
an unusual shark found
off Australia, China,
and Japan. Its skin is
nobbly and fringed like
seaweed, so that it can
lie unseen on the
seabed.

Wobbegong

• The Atlantic trumpetfish is a
clever hunter. Its body is long
and thin, and it hovers
upside down in long
seaweed, swaying so that
tasty shrimps and small
fish mistake it for a
plant.

Trumpetfish

• The bridal burrfish lives on coral
reefs. It has a round body covered in
sharp spikes. When it needs to defend
itself, it inflates into a spiky ball that
makes it look twice its original size.

The ocean depths

Many areas of the ocean are too **deep** for sunlight to reach. Some
creatures have adapted to life in the darkness.

• Some deepsea fish carry their own
lights around, to confuse their
enemies or to attract prey. For
instance, the viperfish has a
luminous pattern along its body.

Viperfish

• The female deepsea
anglerfish has tentacles on
her body. At the tip of each
tentacle there is a shining
lure designed to look like
food for smaller fish. The
anglerfish lies on the
seabed, waiting to gulp
down any unsuspecting
prey.

Anglerfish

Strange but true

• Corals attack each other with stinging
cells, in order to gain more territory.

• Sailors have been
known to mistake
basking whales for
islands and try to land
on them.

• Some tiny male
anglerfish live
permanently attached
to the larger female.

• Giant-sized worms,
crabs, and clams live
near underwater
volcanic ares.

29

Wildlife in the Home

Yοu may not realize it, but you could be sharing your house with wild animals. Houses are good **hunting grounds** and **nesting places** for a variety of creatures, and they provide food stores, too.

Although modern houses tend to be too clean and dry for some pests, it is not unusual to find the occasional beetle, moth, woodlouse, fly, or spider in your home.

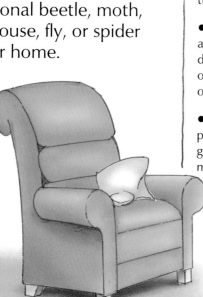

Parasites

Parasites are creatures that depend completely on other animals to survive. They often feed on blood.

- Bed bugs grow to about $\frac{1}{8}$ inch (4 mm) long. By day they hide in warm dark places such as mattresses. At night, they come out to feed on their victim, leaving tiny itchy bites.

- Fleas leave itchy swelling bites. Human fleas are not very common, but cat and dog fleas will occasionally bite people.

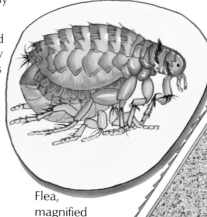

Bed bug, magnified many times

Flea, magnified many times

- If you vacuum your bed mattress regularly, you won't be visited by bed bugs. However, if you have cats or dogs, you will sometimes get a flea.

Furniture and fabric eaters

Some small house creatures like to eat **wood** and **fabric**. They find a perfect supply of food in furniture, carpets, curtains, and clothes.

- Furniture beetles lay their eggs in the crevices of damp wood. When the eggs hatch, the larvae (called woodworm) eat their way to the surface, making tiny tunnels.

- Clothes moths eat feathers, fur, and wool. They live in damp, dark places such as closets and old chests and they lay their eggs on clothes or old carpeting.

- Bookworms are beetle larvae that live on paper. They like damp paper best.

- Woodlice like to eat damp paper. They breathe through gills on their legs. The gills must be kept wet, so woodlice live in damp places.

- Carpet beetles lay their eggs among carpet fluff. When the larvae hatch they are called "woolly bears." They eat feathers, dead insects, fur, and wool.

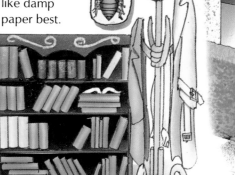

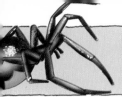

Black widow spider (America): harmful bite | **Termites (America): building damage** | **Scorpions (Africa, S. America): harmful sting**

Hunters

Some house creatures spend their time looking for smaller animals to capture and eat. These **hunters** help to keep the insect population down.

● A house spider's home is usually a sheet of webbing built in a shadowy corner. The spider lives in a silk tube built at the edge of the web. The threads in the web are sticky and trap flying insects, which make the web shake, and the spider then rushes out to kill them.

False scorpion, magnified

● False scorpions often live in house cellars, among piles of damp paper. Although they are small, they are fierce insect hunters.

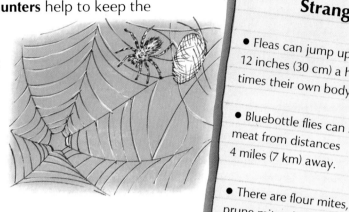

Strange but true

● Fleas can jump up to 12 inches (30 cm) a hundred times their own body length.

● Bluebottle flies can smell meat from distances 4 miles (7 km) away.

● There are flour mites, prune mites, biscuit mites, chocolate mites, and even cheese mites.

● House mice prefer chocolate, nuts, seeds, and cereals to cheese.

Food stealers

Some creatures are out to steal **your food**. An estimated 15 percent of all stored food ends up inside insects or rodents.

● Food mites are about the size of dust specks. They like to live on stale, damp food that is left at room temperature — inside a pantry, for example.

● There are an estimated 3 million bacteria on one housefly. The fly will land on any food it can find, and is likely to leave some bacteria behind when it leaves.

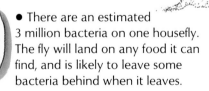

Housefly, magnified

● House mice live in dark, secret places such as lofts and cellars. They like to eat bread and cereals, but they will occasionally eat more unusual items such as soap and candles!

Bed mite, magnified

Silverfish, magnified

● The tiny bed mite eats the scales that constantly fall from human skin. It is widespread but harmless.

● Silverfish are thin, silvery insects about $\frac{1}{3}$ inch (1 cm) long. They live in crevices in bathrooms and kitchens, and come out at night to look for food scraps.

31

Animal Babies

Pregnancies vary in length. Here are some mammal examples:

Golden hamster: two and a half weeks

All animal species produce **new generations**. Most species reproduce when the climate and food supply is right. For instance, many birds hatch new families in spring, when there is plenty of food to eat.

Within the animal kingdom there are many different kinds of **babies** and methods of **giving birth**.

Strange but true

● Gray tree frogs build nests of foam hanging over water. The tadpoles drop out of the foam when they hatch.

● The ichneumon fly injects its eggs into a caterpillar. The larvae hatch and eat their way out.

● Bacteria divide themselves once every 30 minutes or so.

Babies and parents

Some animals are good **parents**, protecting their babies and teaching them survival skills. However, the majority of creatures give no parental care at all.

● Most fish, amphibians, and reptiles lay their eggs and then abandon them. Female fish lay their eggs in the water. Many cannot recognize their own eggs and they often eat them later.

Baby alligator

● The South American discus fish is a good parent. It makes sure that its newborn babies stay close to it for protection, by producing a tasty skin secretion which the babies eat.

● Crocodiles and alligators are caring parents. The female digs a pit, lays her eggs, and then covers them with vegetation. When the babies hatch they squeal at the mother to dig them out.

Discus fish

● Mammal mothers feed and tend their young. For instance, most monkeys carry their babies with them wherever they go. The babies hold on to the mothers' fur.

32

**Guinea pig:
nine weeks**

**Human:
nine months**

**Whale:
one year**

**Elephant:
two years**

● The female midwife toad lays a string of eggs on land. The male then carries the string wrapped around his back legs. When they are ready to hatch he takes the eggs to the water.

Male midwife toad

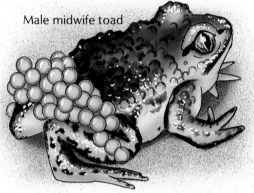

● Young domestic fowl chicks must teach themselves to feed. They begin by pecking at everything on the ground, including their own toes! Gradually they learn which things are the best to eat.

● Some cuckoos do not look after their own chicks. Instead they lay a single egg in a smaller bird's nest. The cuckoo hatches and pushes the other chicks out. Then it takes all the food the unwitting parent brings.

Cuckoo chick

Ways of reproducing

Here are the four basic ways that animals **reproduce**:

● The simplest form of one-celled animals, such as amoebas, reproduce by splitting themselves in half to form two identical creatures. Animals that behave in this way are called asexual.

An amoeba splits in two

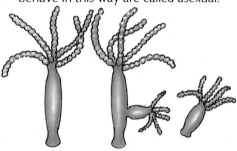

A hydra buds to make a new hydra

● Some simple animals, such as sea corals and freshwater hydra, produce new creatures by "budding." They grow a new branch which is a small version of the parent. Eventually the branch splits off to become a new individual.

● Most animals have different male and female species. The male produces cells called sperm. The female produces egg cells called ova. The male sperm must join with the female egg before a new animal is produced. This method is called sexual reproduction.

Female egg   Male sperm

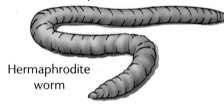

Hermaphrodite worm

● Earthworms and some snails are hermaphrodite. This means that each animal is both male and female, and can produce both sperm and eggs. However, hermaphrodites still have to pair with each other in order to reproduce new creatures.

Eggs and babies

An egg is **fertilized** by a sperm in sexual reproduction. Once this occurs, the egg starts to develop into a new animal.

● Some animals, including most mammals, develop inside their mother's body before they are born. For instance, a newborn foal looks like a miniature version of its parent, and can walk almost immediately.

● Creatures such as birds and many insects lay their eggs once they are fertilized. The babies then develop inside the egg.

Camouflage

Camouflage is a pattern or coloring that **disguises** an animal so that it can hide from enemies, or creep up unseen on prey.

Camouflaged animals blend in with their surroundings. For instance, young deer usually have white spot markings that make them harder to see in the dappled light of a forest.

Some animals, such as the zebra, have vivid skin patterns that blur their outlines and make them hard for predators to see.

Changing color

Some animals can **change color** to match different backgrounds. Here are some examples:

● The Arctic fox, snowshoe rabbit, and ptarmigan live on the Arctic tundra all year round (see p.26). In winter they turn white to blend in with the snow and in summer they change back to darker colors.

Ptarmigan's winter coat

Ptarmigan's summer coat

● The cuttlefish changes color as it swims over different plants and rocks. It has sacs of color pigment in its skin. They expand or contract to produce a wide variety of shades.

Cuttlefish

Master of disguise

The **chameleon** is one of the animal kingdom's masters of disguise. It can change color very quickly.

● The chameleon has color cells called chromatophores in its body. Brain signals make the cells smaller or larger to alter the reptile's skin color.

Chromatophores

Nerves in the spine relay brain signals.

Tricking enemies

These animals fool their enemies by looking like **fiercer creatures**:

● Many butterflies have false eyes on their wings to make them look like a much larger animal.

● The hawkmoth caterpillar is disguised to look like a deadly viper. When it is threatened it puffs itself up to show a false snake's head.

● The king snake is colored with red, yellow, and black rings to make it look like the much deadlier coral snake.

Strange but true

● Sloths let green algae grow on their hair as camouflage.

● A chameleon's color can alter depending on its mood. In general, the calmer it is the paler it is.

● A nightjar on its ground nest looks just like a branch. Unfortunately, its camouflage is so good that it sometimes gets stepped on.

Sea color

Creatures that live in the open sea or in cool waters tend to be dull in color, whilst those that live in warmer waters are often brightly colored. Many have startling patterns, too.

● The sea dragon is camouflaged to mimic seaweed. It has skin extensions which look like the long strands of weed it swims through.

Sea dragon

Stonefish

● The poisonous stonefish lives in warm waters. It has a speckled, lumpy body that enables it to lurk unseen among the stones on the seabed, waiting to grab passing prey.

Insect hide-and-seek

Insects have many enemies, so they are among the most effectively camouflaged creatures in the animal kingdom. They use a variety of different tricks to hide from attackers.

● One species of leaf insect has a flattened body and wings which look exactly like the leaves it feeds on. The disguise is so successful that the leaf insects sometimes try to eat each other!

● The Italian cricket can throw its voice, just like a ventriloquist, so its enemies never know where it is.

● Peppered moths living in polluted cities have turned dark brown. Members of the same species living in the countryside have stayed a speckled white color.

Strange Animals

Male tree frog

Some animals have unique **abilities** or **body parts** that no other species possess. These individual features have usually been developed as ways of helping an animal to survive in one way or another. For instance, many creatures have unusual **defense mechanisms** to surprise their enemies.

Some creatures have unique body parts that help them to **feed** or to **survive** in harsh conditions.

Some animals are so extraordinary that scientists are still baffled by the reasons for their behavior.

Amazing animals

Here are some animals with **unusual skills**:

● The tarsier can turn its head right round to look behind it without moving its body.

Tarsier

● The Texas horned lizard can squirt blood out of its eyes, possibly as a form of defense against enemies.

● When the three-banded armadillo is threatened by enemies, it rolls itself into a very tight armored ball.

Curled-up armadillo

● A gorilla called Koko was taught by humans to use sign language. She used this skill to signal that she wanted a cat as a pet.

Koko the gorilla

Strange but true

● Guillemots can "fly" underwater.

● Flies take off backward.

● It takes an elephant calf six months to learn how to use its trunk.

● Crocodiles sometimes climb up trees.

Texas horned lizard

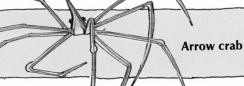
● Most lizards have a tail that can break off if the lizard needs to escape from the grip of a predator. The tail is usually capable of growing again, at least once.

● Giraffes have 18-inch (45-cm) long black tongues which they can use to clean their ears.

Curious connections

Here are some strange animal **similarities**:

● The African elephant's closest relative is the hyrax, which is the size of a rabbit.

● The giraffe has seven neckbones, exactly the same as a human.

Hyrax

Bizarre birds

Here are some unusual patterns of **bird** behavior:

● Once the female Emperor penguin has laid an egg, the male keeps it warm by balancing it on his feet under a flap of skin.

● Some birds, such as the reed warbler, can sing two tunes at once.

Reed warbler

Hummingbird

● The hummingbird is the only bird that can fly backward.

Fascinating fish

The **underwater world** is full of strange surprises:

● The arawana lives in the flooded Amazon rain forest. It can jump up to 6 feet (2 m) out of the water to feed on small birds or bats in the trees above.

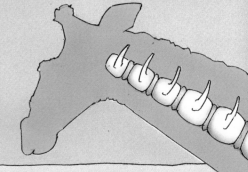

● The African lungfish lives in mud at the bottom of dried-out swamps. It burrows into the ground and covers itself with mucus to keep moist.

● Dolphins, whales, and porpoises talk to each other with clicking and whistling noises.

Endangered Animals

Cuban crocodile

About 5,000 animal species are **endangered**. This means that their numbers are decreasing and that they may die out forever.

An animal species that has disappeared is called **extinct**. The population of some animal species has become so low that they are almost certain to become extinct within the next 20 years.

The endangered panda

Some animals' lives are threatened because their homes and food are being destroyed by **pollution**, **farming**, or **building**. Some are **hunted** for their fur and meat. Sadly, there is a huge illegal trade in "luxury" **animal products** such as rare animal skins and furs.

Land mammals

Although there are organizations to protect endangered wildlife, many animals are still being **poached**, which means that they are killed illegally. Here are some examples:

- The rhinoceros is poached for its horn, which some people believe makes good medicine. Since 1960 the world rhino population has dropped by 85 percent.

- For many years the African elephant was hunted for its ivory tusks, used for jewelry and ornaments. Now the world ivory trade is banned.

Ivory goods

- In Africa, some restaurants serve gorilla steaks. Gorillas are also hunted because they can damage crops. The most endangered species is the mountain gorilla.

- The musk deer is poached for its musk gland, which is used to make perfumes and is said to help treat snake bites.

Marine threat

Harmful chemicals and **oil** find their way into the oceans, making them hazardous for ocean life. Some creatures may escape the pollution, only to become victims of other life-threatening dangers:

- Some countries hunt whales for scientific reasons, but sometimes the carcasses are used illegally for food despite strict hunting laws.

- Many dolphins and other sea creatures die when they are trapped in huge fishing nets.

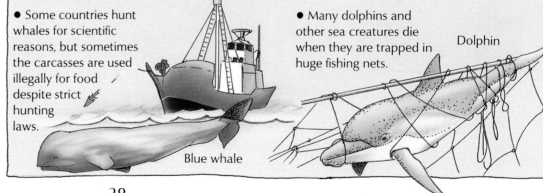

Blue whale

Dolphin

Endangered Animals

Cuban crocodile

About 5,000 animal species are **endangered**. This means that their numbers are decreasing and that they may die out forever.

An animal species that has disappeared is called **extinct**. The population of some animal species has become so low that they are almost certain to become extinct within the next 20 years.

The endangered panda

Some animals' lives are threatened because their homes and food are being destroyed by **pollution**, **farming**, or **building**. Some are **hunted** for their fur and meat. Sadly, there is a huge illegal trade in "luxury" **animal products** such as rare animal skins and furs.

Land mammals

Although there are organizations to protect endangered wildlife, many animals are still being **poached**, which means that they are killed illegally. Here are some examples:

- The rhinoceros is poached for its horn, which some people believe makes good medicine. Since 1960 the world rhino population has dropped by 85 percent.

- For many years the African elephant was hunted for its ivory tusks, used for jewelry and ornaments. Now the world ivory trade is banned.

Ivory goods

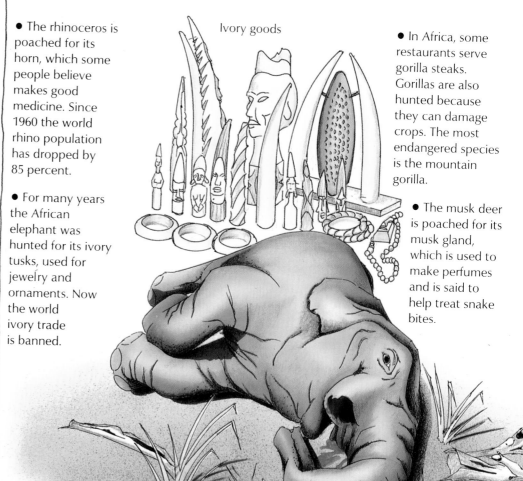

- In Africa, some restaurants serve gorilla steaks. Gorillas are also hunted because they can damage crops. The most endangered species is the mountain gorilla.

- The musk deer is poached for its musk gland, which is used to make perfumes and is said to help treat snake bites.

Marine threat

Harmful chemicals and **oil** find their way into the oceans, making them hazardous for ocean life. Some creatures may escape the pollution, only to become victims of other life-threatening dangers:

- Some countries hunt whales for scientific reasons, but sometimes the carcasses are used illegally for food despite strict hunting laws.

- Many dolphins and other sea creatures die when they are trapped in huge fishing nets.

Dolphin

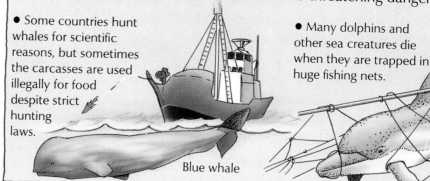

Blue whale

Hatchet fish

Stonefish

Arrow crab

● Most lizards have a tail that can break off if the lizard needs to escape from the grip of a predator. The tail is usually capable of growing again, at least once.

● Giraffes have 18-inch (45-cm) long black tongues which they can use to clean their ears.

Curious connections

Here are some strange animal **similarities**:

● The African elephant's closest relative is the hyrax, which is the size of a rabbit.

● The giraffe has seven neckbones, exactly the same as a human.

Hyrax

Bizarre birds

Here are some unusual patterns of **bird** behavior:

● Once the female Emperor penguin has laid an egg, the male keeps it warm by balancing it on his feet under a flap of skin.

● Some birds, such as the reed warbler, can sing two tunes at once.

Reed warbler

Hummingbird

● The hummingbird is the only bird that can fly backward.

Fascinating fish

The **underwater world** is full of strange surprises:

● The arawana lives in the flooded Amazon rain forest. It can jump up to 6 feet (2 m) out of the water to feed on small birds or bats in the trees above.

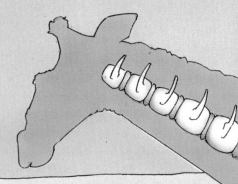

● The African lungfish lives in mud at the bottom of dried-out swamps. It burrows into the ground and covers itself with mucus to keep moist.

●Dolphins, whales, and porpoises talk to each other with clicking and whistling noises.

Sea otter
(Pacific coast)

Snow leopard
(Asia)

Lemur
(Madagascar)

Whooping crane
(North America)

Birds in danger

About one fifth of all the world's endangered species are **birds**. **Oil pollution** causes a large number of bird deaths, but many are **trapped** or **shot** by humans. Protection laws are hard to enforce.

Rare hyacinthine macaws

● Exotic birds are often captured illegally and sold worldwide as caged pets. Amongst the rarest species is the large hyacinthine macaw of the Brazilian rain forest.

A cormorant clogged with oil

● An estimated 300,000 seabirds died when oil was spilt from a tanker off Alaska in 1989.

● Several well-known species of fish may eventually disappear because of overfishing. If shoals are caught more quickly than the fish can reproduce, the numbers decline.

● Many turtles have been forced away from the beaches where they breed, as hotels and tourism take over. Sometimes turtles have been deliberately killed.

Loggerhead turtle

Herring shoal

Strange but true

● In Japan you can buy a pair of real turtleshell glasses for about $2,000.

● Rare African gorillas are sometimes shot so that their hands can be used to make ashtrays.

● When a mother river dugong is killed, the tears of her young are bottled and sold as good luck potion.

39

Saving Animals

All over the world, groups of people are working to **protect** endangered animals and to limit fur, skin, and ivory hunting.

Areas of land called **reserves** have been set aside to provide safe homes for rare animals. There are also underwater nature reserves, where scuba diving and fishing are limited.

Sometimes rare species are kept in **zoos**, where they can safely breed new generations. Occasionally some of these animals are released back into the wild to build up the species once more.

Project tiger

Until recently, the **tiger** was one of the most threatened animal species in the world. In 1972 the Indian government and the Worldwide Fund for Nature launched **Operation Tiger**:

● Tiger reserves were set up across India and Asia to provide safe areas where hunting is banned. Here the animals can breed without disturbance.

● Thanks to the Operation Tiger project, the number of tigers in India alone has more than doubled to over 4,000 since the opening of the reserve areas. The tiger is no longer top of the endangered species list, and numbers are continuing to grow.

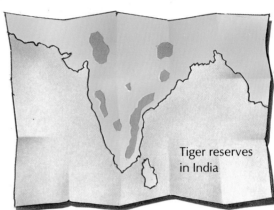

Tiger reserves in India

● Thousands of people pay to visit the reserves every year. The money helps to maintain the land on the reserves and goes towards funding important research.

Bengal tiger

Strange but true

● The rare kakapo parrot lays one egg every four years.

● The coelacanth fish was thought to be extinct for 70 million years, until one was found alive in 1938.

● Insecticide pollution has been traced in the bodies of Antarctic penguins, thousands of miles from civilization.

● The natural habitat of the panda is gradually being destroyed in southwestern China. Wildlife groups are working to create reserves for them along the lines of the Operation Tiger project in India.

Zoo work

● The Arabian oryx became extinct in the wild 20 years ago. Surviving oryx were reared in Arizona, and the species is now back in the wild.

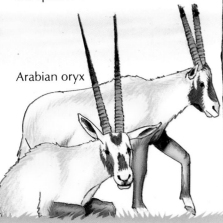

Arabian oryx

● Several endangered monkey species have been bred in zoos. However, it is not always safe to release them back into the wild because their jungle homes are still being destroyed.

● The rare Chatham Island black robin was saved from extinction by New Zealand wildlife experts, who used tom tits to foster the robin chicks.

Chatham Island robin

Extinct animals

An animal is officially **extinct** if it has not been seen for over 50 years. Here are some animals forced into extinction by humans.

● The dodo bird once live on Mauritius. It was killed off in the seventeenth century when humans arrived on the island.

Dodo bird

● The great auk was hunted to extinction in the North Atlantic. It disappeared in the 1500s.

Great auk

● The South African quagga looked like a zebra. It was hunted for food until it died out.

What you can do

Here are some things **you** can do to help protect wildlife:

● Do not buy endangered animal skins or ivory products.

● Never steal birds' eggs from nests.

● Join your local conservation group, to help conserve the wildlife that lives near you.

WWF

Worldwide Fund for Nature badge

Wild Animals Facts and Lists

Wild cats

Wild cats are found in all the continents of the world. This table shows where some wild cats live:

	Asia	Africa	India	China	South America	North America	Europe
Cheetah	●	●					
Hyena	●	●	●	●			
Jaguar					●		
Leopard	●	●					
Lion			●	●			
Lynx	●	●				●	●
Ocelot					●	●	
Puma	●				●	●	
Tiger	●		●				

Endangered and extinct animals

● Scientists believe that up to a third of all known plant and animal species may be extinct by the year 2,500.

● Dinosaurs became extinct about 65 million years ago.

● The North American passenger pigeon was killed for food and became extinct in 1899.

Here are some more endangered animals:

Arabian oryx
Cranes
Crocodiles
Giant tortoises
Golden cats
Indian lions
Lynx
Rhinoceroses

Sand lizards
Spiny anteaters
Tasmanian wolves
The platypus
Tigers
Tragopan pheasants
Wallabies
Whales

The last dodo died in 1681

Pets and wild animals

Some wild animals are now often kept as pets:

The common European tortoise
The Australasian cockatiel
The Australian parakeet
African and Asian waxbills
African and Asian gerbils
South American cavies, or guinea pigs
Asian and North European hamsters
(All present-day golden hamsters in captivity are descended from a litter found in Syria in 1930).

Flightless birds

Here are some examples of birds that cannot fly, even though they have wings:

Emus
Cassowaries
Penguins

Wattlebirds
Ostriches
Kakapo parrots

Burrowing animals

These animals live in burrows:

Mongooses
Aardwolves
Hyenas
Burrowing clams
Fiddler crabs

Congo eels
Moles
Rabbits
Wombats

The foods animals eat

Here are some examples of animals that eat meat only (carnivores):

Anacondas
Crocodiles
Eagles
Komodo dragons

Polar bears
Praying mantis
Tigers
Lions

Here are some animals that eat plants and meat (omnivores):

Baboons
Badgers
Bush babies
Bustards

Cockroaches
Common snapper
Earwigs
Harvestmen spiders

These animals eat carrion (the remains of dead animals):

Carrion Beetles
Golden Eagles

Hyenas
Vultures

Pests

● Pests are creatures that destroy crops or other plants.

● Aphids are insects that carry plant diseases and damage plants by eating them.

● Quelea birds may damage whole fields of grain, partly because of the huge numbers that feed together.

● Locusts are a large kind of grasshopper. Some types of locust are among the world's most destructive pests, flying in huge swarms and eating any plant they land on.

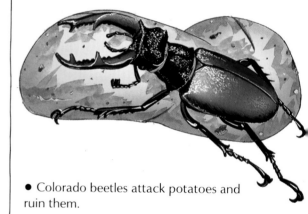

● Colorado beetles attack potatoes and ruin them.

Plant eaters

Here are some examples of animals that eat only plants:

Green turtles
Iguanas
Emus
Gorillas
Rhinoceroses
Zebras
Antelopes
Elephants

Animal communication

Animals communicate with each other so that they can find food, or to attract a mate. This is how some animals communicate:

● Silk moths use their scent to attract a partner.

● Glowworms have a green light that attracts other glowworms.

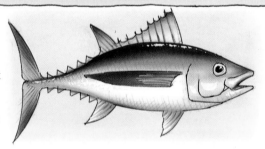

- Mayflies swarm together and "dance" over the water.

- Honey bees do an elaborate dance that directs the other bees to food.

- Ants leave trails to mark the route from their nest so they can return.

- Blue whales make sounds that can be heard by other whales up to 500 miles (850 km) away.

- Squirrelfish make noises that can be heard even out of the water.

- Sticklebacks swim in a zig-zag pattern to attract females.

Changing shape

Here are some examples of animals that go through metamorphosis (change of shape) at different stages in their life:

Earwigs
Grasshoppers
Dragonflies
Butterflies
Moths
Flies

Migration

Some animals migrate (travel from one place to another) at certain times of the year to breed or find food. These are some examples:

- The North American monarch butterfly travels as far as Australia for the winter months.

- Salmon hatch in rivers and migrate to the sea, returning to their birthplace to breed.

- Eels migrate up to 3,500 miles (5,600 km) to reach their breeding grounds.

- Tuna fish travel long distances to reach the Mediterranean where they breed.

- Many birds migrate, but the Arctic tern travels farthest. It flies from the Arctic to the Antarctic, and back again, a trip of 20,000 miles (32,000 km).

Camouflage

Here are some examples of animals that can change color quickly as a way of hiding from their enemies or prey:

Chameleons
Grouper fish
Flatfish
Octopuses
Tree frogs
Blossom spiders

Nighttime animals

Nocturnal animals come out at night to feed or hunt, and rest during the day. These animals are nocturnal:

Many frogs and toads
Coral snakes
The Kakapo parrot
Owls
Nightjars
Opossums

Regrowing limbs

Here are some animals that can regrow parts of their bodies if damaged:

- Starfish can grow new "arms."

- Slowworms can regrow broken-off tails.

- Lizards can grow new tails.

Whales

There are 90 species of whales, dolphins, and porpoises. Here are some whales and their sizes:

Blue whale	100 feet (30 m)
Gray whale	50 feet (15 m)
Sperm whale	42 feet (13 m)
Killer whale	20 feet (6 m)
Pygmy sperm whale	13 feet (4 m)
Narwhal	12 feet (4 m)

Hibernation

- To hibernate means to go into a deep sleep through the winter.

- Newts, hedgehogs, bats, and dormice hibernate over the winter.

- Only two kinds of birds hibernate, and they are both nightjars.

Desert creatures

This is how some desert animals survive:

- Camels store fat in their humps and water in their stomachs.

- The addax antelope does not need to drink very often.

- Jerboas burrow deep underground to keep away from the heat.

- Rhinoceroses bath in muddy water which then dries on them, protecting them from the Sun.

Biggest sea creatures

These are some of the largest creatures to be found in the sea, apart from whales:

Ribbon worm	180 feet (54 m)
Whale shark	60 feet (18 m)
Giant squid	55 feet (17 m)
White shark	40 feet (12 m)
Giant spider crab	12 feet (3.6 m)
Starfish	5 feet (1.5 m)
American lobster	3 feet (1 m)

Dangerous animals

- One golden poison-dart frog could kill up to 1,500 people with its poison.

- The mosquito carries diseases such as malaria, elephantiasis, and yellow fever. Malaria kills over a million people a year.

- The great white shark is the most feared man-eating shark.

43

Wild Animals Facts and Lists

Reptiles

This table shows the average sizes of some reptiles:

Anaconda	30 feet (9 m)
Reticulated python	30 feet (9 m)
Saltwater crocodile	26 feet (8 m)
King cobra	18 feet (5.5 m)
Boa constrictor	14 feet (4.2 m)
Mamba	7 feet (2 m)
Leatherback turtle	6.5 feet (2 m)
Grass snake	3 feet (1 m)
Thread snake	4 inches (114 mm)
Gecko lizard	0.5 inch (17 mm)

This is how long it takes some reptile eggs to hatch:

Grass lizard	42 days
Marine turtle	55 days
Alligator	61 days
Python	61 days
Tortoise	105 days

Amazing eyes

● The giant squid has the largest eyes of any animal. They can be 15 inches (39 cm) across, which is 16 times wider than a human eye.

● A peregrine falcon can spot its prey from more than 5 miles (8 km) away.

● The golden eagle can spot its prey from over 2 miles (3 km) away.

Giant invertebrates

● The bird-eating spider from South America has a body as big as a child's hand.

● The African giant snail measures over 15 inches (390 mm) when fully grown.

● The Borneo dragonfly has a wingspan of 7 inches (190 mm).

Birds

● There are about 100 billion birds in the world.

● There are 9,000 species of birds.

● The ostrich is the tallest bird, at 9 feet (2.74 m).

Fast fliers

Spine-tailed swift	105 mph (170 km/h)
Pigeon	60 mph (96 km/h)
Hawk moth	33 mph (53 km/h)
Monarch butterfly	20 mph (32 km/h)
Honeybee	10 mph (17 km/h)

Beaks

The shape of birds' beaks gives a clue to the food they eat and how they eat it:

Hooked bills	eating flesh
Baggy beaks	scooping fish
Spear beaks	spearing fish
	spearing worms
Parrotbills	cracking seeds
Pointed beaks	spearing insects
	eating seeds
Crossbills	removing seeds from fir cone scales
Chisel beaks	boring nest holes and feeding
Tiny beaks	catching insects in the open mouth while flying

Wing shapes

Hovering birds	small, broad wings
Gliding birds	long, thin wings
Diving birds	wings fold back
Circling birds	long, wide wings
Dodging, diving birds	short, wide wings

Animal nests

Nests are made by many animals in lots of different ways:

● Swans make floating nests of reeds and sticks.

● Sticklebacks make nests using sand and weed.

● Swallows make nests using grasses woven or stuck together with mud and spit.

● Queen bumblebees often use old underground voles' nests in which they make a wax egg chamber.

● Siamese fighting fish make nests out of bubbles, which they hold together like shampoo froth.

● Eagles make the biggest nests. A bald eagle nest found in Florida in 1968 was 10 feet (2.9 m) wide and 20 feet (6 m) deep.

Treetop colonies

These birds make treetop nests in groups:

Crows
Herons
Storks
Pelicans
Weaver birds

Eggs

Here are the biggest and smallest bird egg sizes:

Ostrich	7 inches (177 mm)
Helena's hummingbird	$\frac{1}{2}$ inch (12.7 mm)

● After an egg has been laid, the time it takes to hatch is called its "incubation time."

Egg incubation times:

Finch	12 days
Thrush	14 days
Wren	16 days
Falcon	28 days
Ostrich	42 days
Hawk	44 days
Emperor penguin	63 days
Royal albatross	79 days

Animal sizes

These are the heights of some animals:

Giraffe	18 ft. (5 m)
African elephant	10 ft. (3 m)
Ostrich	9 ft. (2.7 m)
Brown bear	8 ft. (2.4 m)

Weights

Animal weights, from smallest to largest:

Bee hummingbird	0.05 oz. (1.4 g)
Mouse	0.8 oz. (22 g)
Goliath beetle	3 oz. (85 g)
Rat	16 oz. (455 g)
Marmoset	1.5 lb. (0.7 kg)
Ringtail monkey	6 lb. (2.7 kg)
Otter	13 lb. (6 kg)
Armadillo	13.5 lb. (6.2 kg)
Ocelot	42 lb. (19 kg)
Porpoise	103 lb. (47 kg)
Cheetah	127 lb. (57 kg)
Alligator	127 lb. (57 kg)
Llama	375 lb. (170 kg)
Polar bear	700 lb. (320 kg)
Moose	800 lb. (360 kg)
Pilot whale	1,500 lb. (680 kg)
Walrus	3,500 lb. (1,620 kg)
African elephant	15,700 lb. (7,100 kg)
Sperm whale	83,000 lb. (37,600 kg)
Blue whale	344,000 lb. (156,000 kg)

Animal pregnancies

This is how long some babies take to grow inside their mothers before they are born:

Opossum	13 days
House mouse	19 days
Chimpanzee	237 days
Camel	406 days
Giraffe	410 days
Rhinoceros	560 days
Indian elephant	624 days

Animal speeds

● The slowest land mammal is the three-toed sloth of tropical South America. Its average speed is 7 feet (2.13 m) a minute.

● The sleepiest mammals are armadillos, sloths, and opposums. They spend 80 percent of their lives sleeping or dozing.

Animal lifespans

This is how long some animals live:

Mayfly	1 day
Mouse	2–3 yrs
Rattlesnake	18 yrs
Lion	25 yrs
Hippopotamus	40 yrs
Ostrich	50 yrs
African elephant	60 yrs
Dolphin	65 yrs
Rhinoceros	70 yrs
Turtle	100 yrs

Animal skins

● Snakes and lizards have scaly skins. The rough scales underneath help a snake to move along. The skin is watertight, enabling snakes and lizards to live in or out of the water.

● Tortoises have developed their scaly skin into an armored shell.

● Furry or feathered skins keep some animals warm in winter.

● Birds lose some of their feathers in the summer to keep cool.

● Birds such as penguins oil their feathers from an oil gland in their skin to waterproof themselves.

Animal feet

● Swans and ducks have webbed feet which they use as paddles when swimming.

● The blue-footed booby uses its webbed feet to incubate its eggs during breeding.

● Lizards, newts, gorillas, and lemurs are examples of animals that have five toes on each foot. Toes are used for climbing and gripping.

● The elephant's foot is also five-toed, but is round and massive to support its weight.

History of how life began

The development of animals and plants has taken millions of years. The facts below show this evolution as if it had happened in a year.

● January 1: the Earth forms.

● March 29: bacteria and other simple life forms appear.

● November 27: the first fish develop in the sea.

● December 15: the first dinosaurs appear.

● December 28: various mammals develop.

● December 31: the first ape-men appear. Modern humans develop just hours before the end of the year.

INDEX